W9-AEC-051

DON'T STEP ON THE FOUL LINE

SPORTS SUPERSTITIONS

GEORGE SULLIVAN

The Millbrook Press
Brookfield, Connecticut

Published by The Millbrook Press, Inc.
2 Old New Milford Road
Brookfield, Connecticut 06804
www.millbrookpress.com

Library of Congress Cataloging-in-Publication Data
Sullivan, George, 1933–
Don't step on the foul line : sports superstitions / George
Sullivan ; illustrated by Anne Canevari Green.
p. cm.
Includes index.
Summary: Describes a variety of superstitions observed by
athletes in such sports as baseball, hockey, tennis, and foot-
ball.
ISBN 0-7613-1558-6 (lib. bdg.)
1. Baseball players—Attitudes—Juvenile literature. 2.
Superstition—Juvenile literature. [1. Sports—Folklore.
2. Superstition.] I. Green, Anne Canevari, ill. II. Title.
GV863.A1 S893 2000
796.357—dc21 00-021483

introduction

"Honestly, I don't have any super-stitions," Bill Madlock, a lifetime .300 hitter with the Cubs, Pirates, and several other major-league baseball teams, once said.

ATTENTION, LADIES AND GENTLEMEN ... MIKE WITSKI WILL NOT BE IN THE LINEUP TONIGHT — HIS PREGAME RITUALS TOOK SO LONG THAT HE MISSED THE PLANE .

But after he thought about it for a moment or two, Madlock admitted that if he didn't tap home plate with his bat three times before the pitch, he couldn't hit. And he would always walk behind the umpire when getting into the batter's box.

Madlock also conceded that when he wanted to warm up his throwing arm, he always sought out a teammate who was hitting well.

Bill Madlock was not unusual. Routines and rituals, and charms and omens, are as much a part of sports as sweating and chewing gum.

Most athletes don't like to admit they're superstitious, however. Question a player about what seems to be an unusual habit, and he or she is likely to shrug and say, "Sure, I do things in a certain way every day. But I'm not superstitious. I just have a 'routine.'"

Other players call them "habits" or "procedures." Whatever they're called, it comes down to the same thing—superstition.

Superstition is a belief or practice that is not based upon any law of nature or anything else that is true or reasonable. Believing that 13 is an unlucky number is a common superstition. But there is no logical reason to believe that 13 is any different from 9 or 14 or any other number.

Why are people superstitious? Why do they carry lucky charms or believe in the power of certain numbers?

A superstition is a crutch, a prop. It helps to get one through a difficult situation. It helps to relieve anxiety.

This is particularly true in sports. Take baseball, for instance. Because pitched or batted balls travel uncertain paths, a player is never sure what's going to happen in a game. A pebble in the infield or a bad call by an umpire can affect the outcome of a crucial game.

There is also the fear factor, the anxiety a batter experiences at the idea of facing a 95-mile (153-km) per hour fastball. A batting helmet helps to ease the fear. Some athletes believe that tapping home plate three times or taping a lucky penny in a shoe is also helpful.

"Superstitious behavior helps athletes prepare for a game," says an article in *Psychology Today*, "and gives them a sense of control over weather, injury, and bad luck."

A scientific study has shown this to be true for all people. Years ago, anthropologist Bronislaw Malinowski studied the people of the Trobriand Islands off the coast of eastern New Guinea. He found that islanders who fished in the lagoon, where there was little danger and plenty of fish, got by on their skills. But those who fished in the open ocean, where danger lurked and fish were fewer, turned to superstitious practices to help them.

Each sport has its own superstitions. Baseball players are superstitious about stepping on the foul lines or certain bases. The great Willie Mays, for instance, always stepped on first base on his way to his position in the outfield.

who's superstitious? who isn't?

The more important the event, the more likely the participants are to rely on superstitions. During spring training in baseball and in preseason football games, players don't pay much attention to superstitions. But in the World Series or Super Bowl, it is a very different story.

That's one of the findings of several of the dozen or so studies of athletes that have been conducted by university professors in the United States and Canada.

According to the studies, age and experience relate to superstition. The older the players and the longer they have played as first-stringers, the more likely they are to be superstitious.

This is true because superstitious behavior is usually learned from one's teammates. Thus the older, more experienced player has been exposed to superstitious conduct for a longer period of time.

Another finding declares that winning teams are more likely to be superstitious than losing ones. That's because success leads to the development of routines and patterns of behavior. If you do something and your team wins, you do it again.

The reverse is also true—poor teams don't pursue superstitions. As one college baseball player put it, "If you're so bad that you can't do anything to win, who cares about superstitions?"

Hockey players, who use more equipment than players in most other sports, have assorted superstitions concerning it.

Tapping the goalie on the pads or tapping the goalposts before a game are common rituals.

Basketball players, who wear much less gear, are likely to develop superstitions that have to do with the ball or with one another. They bounce the ball a certain number of times before a free throw. They stack hands; they slap hands.

Do superstitions really "work" for an athlete? Can putting a double knot in one's shoelaces or always wearing the same T-shirt help an athlete perform better?

It's not likely. But a superstitious practice can be a way of coping with the anxiety of competition. It can lessen stress; it can help to calm you down.

And if you're feeling comfortable and secure, you'll probably play better. As a result, many players believe that superstitious practices seem to work.

"I think it has absolutely no bearing on how you perform," professional golfer Val Skinner once noted. "But if it gives you a feeling that it is going to make a difference, why not do it?"

Why not, indeed?

Fill your pockets with lucky charms or pin them to your uniform. Always eat the same food before a game. Keep a teddy bear in your gear bag. Never step on a foul line. *Never!*

But also work to develop your skills, listen to your coach, and practice hard. Just in case.

hat trick

For the Minnesota Twins, it was a nightmare. Leading the Boston Red Sox, 6–1, in the seventh inning of an early-season game in 1987, the Twins saw Boston score seven runs in the eighth inning to edge into the lead, 8–6.

Keith Atherton shut out the Red Sox in the top of the ninth inning. When the Twins came to bat, Al Newman sparked a Minnesota comeback. He did it by shouting out, "Rally Hats! Rally Hats!"

His teammates flew into action, turning their caps inside out and placing them sideways on their heads.

It worked. Gary Gaetti stepped to the plate to start the ninth inning for the Twins and smacked a home run into the left-field seats. That cut the Red Sox lead to one run.

"I got back to the dugout, started shaking hands, and noticed that everybody had on their Rally Hats," Gaetti later told reporters. "I love it! I tell you, I'm not above doing stuff like that."

One out later, Tom Brunansky hit another home run, which tied the game.

After Keith Atherton blanked the Red Sox in the top of the tenth inning, it was Rally Hats time again.

It worked again. Dan Gladden, the leadoff hitter, singled. Then Kent Hrbek, who had been in a hitting slump, blasted a homer that gave the Twins a 10–8 victory.

Afterward, there were people who brushed aside the idea that the Rally Hats had anything to do with the Twins' victory. They said it was just one of those silly baseball superstitions. But to the Twins, who went on to win the World Series that season, there was nothing silly about it.

all-time favorite

It's the most visible superstition in baseball. Players, coaches, and managers at every level of the game from Little League to the

major leagues step over the foul line on trips to and from the dugout to the infield or outfield.

Mel Stottlemyre, a star pitcher with the New York Yankees and later the team's pitching coach, was one of the countless players who avoided the foul line. He once explained why: "We were playing the Twins, and I was headed for the bullpen to warm up before the start of the game. I made it a point not to step on the foul line, and Jim Hegan, a Yankee coach, said that I shouldn't be superstitious, that I shouldn't be afraid to step on the line.

"So I did.

"The first batter I faced was Ted Uhlaender, and he hit a line drive off my left shin. It went for a hit. Then Rod Carew, Tony Oliva, and Harmon Killebrew followed with base hits. The fifth man hit a single. I was charged with five runs.

"I never stepped on a foul line again."

Some players and coaches follow the ritual throughout their careers. It's as normal as wearing socks. A sportswriter once asked Sparky Anderson, manager of the Detroit Tigers, why he avoided the line. "I picked up the habit in high school," Anderson said, "and it's too late to change now."

Frank Lucchesi, who once managed the Texas Rangers, had a mania about foul lines. He was so nutty about jumping over them that his players made up a nickname for him. They called him "Hippity Hop."

A handful of players do exactly the opposite; they purposely step on the line. Catcher Darrell Porter, a catcher for the St. Louis Cardinals, Texas Rangers, and a couple of other teams, always made it a point to avoid the lines. Then one day he accidentally stepped on a line, and nothing bad happened to him. That led to a different routine. On the opening day of each season, when the players were being introduced to the fans, Porter made it a point to mash the foul line with both feet.

blighted bus

Late one May night in 1992, after the final game of a three-game series against the Yankees in New York, the California Angels boarded a pair of buses for the three-hour ride south to Baltimore, where they were to play the Orioles the next day. So began a trip that was to end in what was perhaps the worst disaster of the season.

The buses, designated Bus 1 and Bus 2, eased their way through the traffic outside Yankee Stadium, then headed across the George Washington Bridge and onto the New Jersey Turnpike. At first, the trip was uneventful. Some players dozed; others read. In Bus 1, some watched a Chuck Norris movie on the television screen.

Without warning, misfortune struck. Manager Buck Rodgers, sitting in the front seat on the right side of Bus 1, later recalled hitting some bumps in the road. Then he turned to see Frank Sims, the team's traveling secretary, standing in the aisle and shouting.

When Rodgers turned back to look out the front window, he could see the driver had lost control going around a curve. The bus plunged down a hill, and tree limbs started breaking the windshield glass. Rodgers slid down to the floor. When the bus struck a final tree and crashed, Rodgers suffered a broken knee, a smashed elbow, two broken ribs, and a broken wrist.

Several other members of the team were also injured, though none as seriously as Rodgers. Players aboard Bus 2 arrived within minutes to help. "Everyone was super," Rodgers later recalled.

Rodgers spent more than two weeks in the hospital and several months at home recovering from his injuries. The team never got back on the track that season after the accident and was to finish in fifth place in the Western Division of the American League.

On August 21, just three months to the day after the crash, the Angels again wound up a three-game series at Yankee Stadium. They were scheduled to take the same bus ride to Baltimore that had ended in disaster. But the players declared publicly that the buses were not to be designated Bus 1 and Bus 2. Instead, they were to be known as Bus 2 and Bus 3.

P.S.: The buses arrived in Baltimore safely.

hit song

Like many teams in professional and college sports, the Philadelphia Flyers of the National Hockey League always played *The Star-Spangled Banner* before home games at the Spectrum. But on the evening of December 11, 1969, the club pulled a switch. Instead of playing a recording of the national anthem, the club invited Kate Smith, a well-known singer, to sing *God Bless America*, a song for which she was famous, before a game. That night the Flyers won.

Smith was asked to sing *God Bless America* again, and the team won again. The Flyers then started inviting Smith back to sing before important games.

On May 19, 1974, when the Flyers played the Boston Bruins in the final playoff game of the season, Smith was there to sing *God Bless America*. The Flyers won, 1–0, to capture the Stanley Cup. The Flyers won the Stanley Cup again in 1975, with Smith performing before a semifinal game at the Spectrum. In professional hockey, winning the Stanley Cup is similar to winning baseball's World Series or pro football's Super Bowl.

In the years that followed, when Smith could not appear at Philadelphia home games to sing *God Bless America*, the club would play her recording of the song. Of course, the Flyers didn't win every game, but her record with the team was impressive. As a result, Kate Smith became a Philadelphia institution, like the Liberty Bell or Constitution Hall.

Kate Smith died in 1986. After that, the Flyers continued the tradition by sometimes playing a recording of her *God Bless America*. "We use it for our home openers and during the playoffs," said a

team spokesperson. Although the recording doesn't cast quite the magic spell that Kate Smith herself once did, the song never fails to bring back warm memories.

tennis tactics

Martina Navratilova, a dominant figure in women's tennis through the 1980s and into the 1990s, always wore the same pair of diamond earrings during a tournament. She wouldn't think of stepping out on the court without them. And on the final day of a tournament, Navratilova always wore a greenish blue tennis dress.

Navratilova was not unusual—tennis players are among the most superstitious of all athletes. Maybe it's because tennis pits a single player against another and produces great tension as a result. A superstitious practice can help to relieve that tension.

Many tennis superstitions involve balls. Dick Stockton, once one of the pro game's top ten players, refused to use the same ball after he had served a fault or a let. "I had to punish that ball by not using it," Stockton said.

Onetime U.S. Girls' champion Lisa Bonder, if she won a point, liked to use the same ball for the next point. But her chief superstitions concerned clothing and food. If she had a good tournament, Bonder would wear the same outfits during the next tournament. And when she was playing well, she always ate the same breakfast—a toasted bagel with jam, and hot chocolate with extra whipped cream.

Ivan Lendl, a three-time winner of the U.S. Open, was willing to vary what he ate, as long as his meals were served in the same restaurant. Lendl didn't like to change his eating place once a tournament began.

Sweden's Bjorn Borg, one of the sport's all-time greats, had the odd habit of refusing to return to his hotel for anything once he had left for a match. This even applied to his rackets. On the rare occasions when he forgot them in his room, Borg would send a friend to fetch them.

lucky takeout

During the time the Washington Redskins spent in San Diego, California, preparing for Super Bowl XXII in 1988, Washington coach Joe Gibbs told the press his team wasn't superstitious. Gibbs wasn't being completely honest, however. He was overlooking Washington's lucky doughnuts.

For eleven years, Montgomery Donuts, a Rockville, Maryland, bakery, had been supplying the Redskins with doughnuts for team

NOW I GET THE CHOCOLATE, CHUCK AND MIKE GET THE TOASTED COCONUT...

breakfasts before games. Gibbs, taking no chances, arranged with the company to have ten dozen doughnuts flown out to San Diego for the team's breakfast before the Super Bowl.

The Washington order included three dozen honey dip, two dozen raised chocolate, two dozen honey wheat, one dozen toasted coconut, and half a dozen each of chocolate cake, plain cake, and a cream-filled doughnut called "black cat."

Quarterback Doug Williams, whose pinpoint passing helped the Redskins overwhelm the Denver Broncos, 42–10, and who earned the game's Most Valuable Player award, preferred honey dip doughnuts.

lucky chew

Most athletes chew gum. Some say it helps them to relax. Others chew to help keep their mouths moist. Wide receiver Fred Biletnikoff of the Oakland Raiders, whose timely receptions earned him the Super Bowl Most Valuable Player award in Super Bowl XI in 1977, chewed gum for superstitious reasons.

For every game, Biletnikoff followed a plan. He chewed three sticks of gum at a time. He might start a game with two sticks of peppermint and one of Juicy Fruit. If the Raiders played well, he'd stick with that combination.

But if the Raiders failed to move the ball and make a first down, Biletnikoff would change the mix. He might switch to a wad of Double Bubble and a couple of cinnamon Chiclets.

Biletnikoff had help in performing his gum-chewing ritual. Dick Romanski, the team's equipment manager, stood watch over Biletnikoff's gum supply. When new brands and new flavors were

required, Romanski unwrapped each piece in the proper order and popped them one by one into Biletnikoff's mouth. Otherwise, said Biletnikoff, the routine would never have worked.

faster than a speeding bullet

Ken Kravec, a pitcher with the Chicago White Sox during the 1970s, engaged in a superstitious practice that never failed to draw grins from his teammates. Whenever he left the dugout to go out to the mound to begin an inning, Kravec would stand up and grip the front of his jacket with both hands, and then literally rip it off, just as if he were Clark Kent transforming himself into Superman.

Superstitious Coach

Players aren't the only ones who are superstitious. Coaches can be, too.

Take for example, Chris—for Christine—Weller, who, in 1999, began her twenty-fifth season as head coach of women's basketball at the University of Maryland. It seems that during the 1984–1985 season, the Terrapins finished with a losing record—and no player was wearing No. 12. This bothered Coach Weller. As soon as she restored a No. 12 to the lineup, the Terps resumed their winning ways.

During games, fans who watch are aware of some of her other superstitions. For good luck, she'll often tap her knuckles against her head three times and then knock on the floor three times. She also has a favorite pregame ritual. When there is precisely 1 minute, 12 seconds on the clock before the start of a game, she'll call the players together, then clap her hands and yell out, "Let's go, Terps!" She follows exactly the same routine before the start of the second half.

"I have no idea how that started," she says.

Weller earned her reputation for being superstitious during her first year at Maryland, when she was an assistant coach. She became known for wearing the same outfit for every game.

"I planned that," she says. "I said I was superstitious because I had only three outfits that I could possibly wear. Then once we started winning, I kept wearing the same outfit."

Penny Power

Athletes who wear lucky charms around their necks or carry them in their pockets are following a tradition that dates from primitive times. The first charms, or amulets, were seeds or nuts of unusual shape or color. The acorn, for example, was supposed to possess powers that helped to assure long life. It was as popular in ancient times as the four-leaf clover is today.

Ancient people also used animal claws, teeth, and bones as amulets. A warrior who wore a string of tiger teeth around his neck believed that he would enjoy tigerlike strength and ferocity.

When it comes to charm-wearing among modern-day professional athletes, baseball players beat all others. Take Tito Fuentes, who had a long career as an infielder with the San Francisco Giants and several other teams. Fuentes wore a dozen or more gold chains around his neck for good luck. Before stepping into the batter's box, he always took time to arrange the chains, making sure they were in perfect alignment under his uniform.

More typical was Dave Parker, a noted slugger for the Cincinnati Reds. One day Parker received an envelope containing a

letter and a shiny penny. The penny had once belonged to a friend of Parker's who had been using it for luck. "The coin carried me through World War II," the friend wrote, "and I've survived seven heart operations. Rub the coin when you need help, and it will respond."

Parker rubbed it and rubbed it—and went on a 13-game hitting streak. During the streak, he had 21 hits in 54 at bats (for a .389 average), with 3 home runs and 16 runs batted in.

Parker took the penny to a Cincinnati jeweler and had a chain attached to it so he could wear it around his neck. It looked like almost any other piece of jewelry, and certainly didn't attract the attention that a string of acorns or a necklace of tiger teeth might have.

sports zoo

A mascot, as defined in dictionaries, is an animal, person, or thing that is supposed to bring good luck. Almost all high-school, college, and professional teams have adopted mascots to represent their teams.

What are the most popular mascots? Almost all come from the animal world. According to *What's in a Nickname? Exploring the Jungle of College Athletic Mascots*, the most common are eagles, taken by seventy-two college teams. Tigers are also very popular, adopted by sixty-eight teams. Other frequently seen mascots are cougars and bulldogs.

Devils are popular, too. There are eleven devils: seven are black; four are red.

The devils, however, are balanced by twenty-one saints, two preachers, one friar, and one parson.

Some mascots are unusual. The teams at the University of California at Irvine are called Anteaters.

At Whittier College in Whittier, California, the teams are known as the Poets. This makes sense, since the college was named in honor of John Greenleaf Whittier, a noted American poet of the nineteenth century.

At Nazareth College in Kalamazoo, Michigan, the teams are called the Moles. This has to be explained. At Nazareth, the campus is often covered in deep snow during the winter. To make it easier to get around, belowground passageways connect the dorms, classrooms, and administrative buildings. After a while, everyone must get to feel like one of the small, insect-eating animals with tiny eyes and velvety fur that spend most of their lives underground.

Superstitious Superstar

Third baseman Wade Boggs of the Tampa Bay Devil Rays took his place among baseball's all-time great hitters when he stroked the 3,000th hit of his career in 1999. He was only the 23rd player to reach that plateau.

A left-handed batter, Boggs was a hitting marvel from the very beginning of his major-league career. He batted .349 in his rookie year of 1982, and he won the first of his five American League batting titles in 1983, hitting .361.

Boggs wasn't notable for just his batting skill. Year in, year out, he was a league leader in superstitious practices.

Boggs had more than eighty rituals that he followed. Eating chicken was the most important of them.

Boggs ate chicken every day of the week during the season, whether his team was playing at home or on the road. It was not only because he considered chicken to be nutritious and economical. "There are base hits in chicken!" he declared.

Boggs traced the magic power of chicken to 1977, when he was playing in the minor leagues in Winston-Salem, North

Carolina. Boggs wasn't earning much money then. "We were eating chicken four times a week," Boggs once recalled, "because it was cheap and fit into our budget."

Boggs's wife, Debbie, also remembered that period. "On the days that he ate chicken, he seemed to get more hits," she said. "I'd serve pork chops to give him a break from chicken, but he didn't do as well."

The real turning point came during spring training in 1982, which was Boggs's rookie season. He was then playing for the Boston Red Sox. One night, not long before a game against the St. Louis Cardinals, Boggs sat down to lemon chicken, one of his favorite dishes. That night he got five hits in six trips to the plate. He also became hooked for all time on chicken.

Boggs soon became well known for his preference for chicken. There were countless newspaper stories and television features about him and his favorite food.

Because of the publicity, Boggs's fan mail often included chicken recipes. At one time, according to Debbie Boggs, the couple was receiving more than one hundred recipes a week.

Boggs, Debbie, and his mother got all the best recipes together and put out a cookbook. It told how to prepare lemon chicken, chicken and rice, chicken and dumplings, olive chicken, Italian chicken, and scores of other chicken dishes. The book was titled *Fowl Tips*.

Another of Boggs's superstitious practices had to do with the ancient *chai* symbol. (*Chai* is the Hebrew word for "life.") The symbol looks like this:

Every time he stepped to the plate, Boggs would draw the *chai* symbol in the dirt with his bat.

Boggs, who was born in Omaha, Nebraska, and brought up in Tampa, Florida, learned about the *chai* when he was 13. He came upon a drawing of the symbol in a magazine and decided to use it to help his hitting.

"It must have worked," Boggs once told *The Boston Jewish Times*, "because I've been doing it ever since."

Boggs followed another superstitious practice before he even got to the plate. When he was in the on-deck circle, he would carefully arrange the pine-tar rag, the weighted batting doughnut, and the powdered rosin bag in a precise way. Then he would use each of them in exactly the same order on each turn at bat.

Throughout his long career, Boggs was enchanted by the number 17. When he signed his contract with the Red Sox for 1984, Boggs asked not for $700,000 or $725,000, but $717,000. (He got it.)

Before each game, Boggs would run in the outfield to loosen up. There was nothing superstitious about that. It was *when* he ran that mattered. Whenever his team was playing a night game, Boggs always ran at precisely the same time: 7:17 P.M.

Of course, by 7:17 Boggs had eaten his meal of chicken. He liked hot dogs, too, and would sometimes have two or three before a game. During the off-season, Boggs would switch to fish for many of his meals. Once spring training began, however, it was back to chicken every day.

Boggs's family, friends, and teammates accepted his bizarre conduct without a word. After all, if you're a baseball superstar, a player talented enough to get 3,000 hits during your career, you can do most anything you want without drawing any comment.

Customs, quirks, and odd habits

When Ron Kittle, who played for the Chicago White Sox and a couple of other American League teams, was a Little Leaguer, his dad taught him to use his foot to draw a line in the dirt in the batter's box parallel to the inside edge of home plate. His dad felt that the line would help young Ron in learning the mechanics of hitting.

Kittle learned to hit well enough to become a Rookie of the Year and a slugger of some note. But he never stopped drawing that line.

"It's probably a superstition now more than anything else," he said. "But I wouldn't feel comfortable without it. That line is very important to me."

Countless other athletes have superstitious rituals they perform during competition. While they may not always date from childhood, as Kittle's did, they treat them very seriously. For instance:

- Wolfgang Suhnholz, of the Los Angeles Aztecs of the old North American Soccer League, always threw away his socks after playing a losing game.

- Professional golfer Alice Miller refused to kill any bugs she encountered on the course. If one interfered with her shot, she would carefully pick it up and move it.

- Before every game at the Hoosier Dome, wide receiver Matt Bouza of the Indianapolis Colts always spit his gum into the

same drainpipe on the field. On road trips, Bouza never unpacked his suitcase.

- Pitcher Mark (the "Bird") Fidrych of the Boston Red Sox, who is remembered for talking to baseballs while on the mound, had a curious superstition. Whenever someone got a hit off him, Fidrych treated the ball as if there were something wrong with it and threw it out of the game.

- Mary Lou Retton, a gold-medal winner in the Olympic Games, used the same shampoo before every gymnastics competition.

- Melissa Belote, a world champion in the backstroke, carried a stuffed frog to every swim meet and placed it on the starting blocks before her event.

- It's not just baseball players who avoid white lines. Tennis star John McEnroe avoided stepping on the lines of the court whenever it was his turn to serve.

- Figure skater Peggy Fleming, another Olympic gold medalist, always had to put her left foot into her tights first and to lace and tie her left skate before the right.

- All-Pro defensive tackle Jack Youngblood of the Los Angeles Rams always chewed five pieces of gum during a game. "No more, no less, always five," he said.

- Charlie Waters, a defensive back for the Dallas Cowboys, was known to have a helmetful of superstitious practices. Asked to name them, he'd reply, "My biggest superstition is that I don't tell what my superstitions are. If I did, they'd lose their power."

time killer

Mike Hargrove, a first baseman with the Cleveland Indians, used to drive opposing teams crazy with the long ritual he went through every time he came to the plate. Hargrove would step out of the batter's box, prop his bat up against one thigh, then rub his hands together, tug at one sleeve, tug at the other, tug at one batting glove, tug at the other, hitch up his belt, adjust his cap, and so on. And he would go through the routine on every pitch.

Even Hargrove's teammates would get annoyed by his conduct. They came up with a good nickname for him. They called him the "Human Rain Delay."

rope trick

Wearing a good-luck medal around one's neck or carrying a lucky coin in one's pocket are common practices. But charms can take any number of forms. Often they're personal and unique.

Take, for instance, Mike Andrews, second baseman for the Boston Red Sox. One day, as Andrews took his position in the infield, he saw a couple of strands of tattered rope. They had come from the drag the ground crew used to smooth the infield. Andrews picked up the pieces and stuffed them in his pocket. He got two hits that day.

The next day, the same thing happened. Andrews found two pieces of rope near his infield position, stuck them in his pocket, and got two hits.

The third day, Andrews told himself that he was being foolish. He didn't pick up any rope; he didn't get any hits, either.

From that day on, Andrews always searched for rope. "I must have looked like a wacko out there, looking around for rope strands," he once recalled.

The next season, disaster struck. The Red Sox ground crew switched from a rope drag to a new metal one. Andrews had a batting slump that lasted the entire season.

Creature of habit

A ritual, according to dictionaries, is any pattern of behavior that one keeps repeating. When it comes to superstitious habits, few athletes are the equal of Steve Preece, a defensive back with the Los Angeles Rams. In fact, Preece was a Hall of Famer when it came to rituals.

On the day of a game, Preece's routine would begin at breakfast, when he ate, as he termed it, "a giant meal." It included bran cereal, wheat bread, two or three poached eggs, and an assortment of vitamin pills. The meal was always the same.

After breakfast, Preece would always leave for the stadium at exactly the same time—11:20 A.M.

Before the game began, Preece would eat a candy bar every hour on the hour. His favorites were Nestlé's Crunch and Hershey's chocolate—plain, no almonds.

When he dressed, every item of clothing had to go on from left to right. Preece had his left ankle taped first, then his right. His wrists were taped left first, then right. He put on his socks in the same order, always the left foot first. He stepped into his pants left foot first.

When his team took the field and began warm-up exercises, Preece would do only two or three of them with the other players. Then, as the team headed back to the locker room, Preece would go off into a corner of the stadium and do ten push-ups by himself.

Later, while the national anthem was being played, Preece never failed to make sure that he was standing on his team's 49-yard line.

In one of his seasons with the Rams, the team won their conference championship, then faced the Dallas Cowboys in a playoff game. The Rams trailed, 17–16, as the game came down to the final minutes.

The Cowboys had the ball. Quarterback Roger Staubach pedaled back to pass. He surveyed the field, then fired to Drew Pearson. Preece, eager to intercept, darted in front of the Dallas receiver.

But when the ball arrived and the two struggled for it, Pearson snatched it away and raced all the way to the end zone. The touchdown doomed the Rams. The Cowboys won, 27–16.

Afterward, Preece was asked about the key play. What had happened? Did he misjudge Staubach's throw? Or did Pearson outmuscle him?

Preece shook his head. "No," he said, "It was the first game since high school that I didn't wear eye black."

the real hero

The Time: October 25, 1986

The Place: Shea Stadium, New York City

The Event: The World Series, the New York Mets vs. the Boston Red Sox, Game No. 6

It has been called the most exciting game in baseball history. The Red Sox had won three of the first five Series games. When they scored twice in the tenth inning of the sixth game to edge ahead, 5–3, it seemed certain that they were about to claim the world championship.

In the bottom of the tenth, the Mets players watched in silence as Wally Backman hit a fly ball to left field that was an easy out. Then Keith Hernandez flied out to center.

The Mets had one out left. The Red Sox players were poised on the dugout steps, ready to dash onto the field to congratulate their teammates.

But Gary Carter delayed the celebration by singling to left field. Kevin Mitchell followed with another base hit to center field. Then Ray Knight delivered a single, sending Carter home and the tying run to third base. Mets fans were on their feet and screaming.

Bob Stanley came in from the bullpen to replace Red Sox pitcher Calvin Schiraldi. Mookie Wilson strode to the plate. With the count 2 and 2 on Wilson, Stanley fired a wild pitch. Mitchell raced home, and Knight went to second. Now the score was tied.

On the next pitch, Wilson hit a slow grounder. It trickled down the first base line and through the legs of first baseman Bill Buckner. Knight streaked home from second base with the winning run. The next night, the Mets capped their amazing comeback by winning the seventh game of the Series and the championship.

Who was the Mets' hero? Some said Gary Carter, whose base hit had started the rally in Game 6. Others pointed to Ray Knight and Kevin Mitchell, who had also delivered key hits. Still others named Keith Hernandez. Why ? The reasons were not the usual ones.

After making the second out in the tenth inning, Hernandez left the dugout, then made his way through the team's dressing room and into manager Davey Johnson's office. He sat behind Johnson's desk and watched the game on television.

When the Mets began getting hits, Hernandez thought about returning to the dugout to be with his teammates. But he remained just where he was. He didn't want to break the spell. "There are hits and runs in this chair," Hernandez thought. Not until the winning run had crossed the plate did Hernandez dare to get up.

Hernandez later admitted that such rituals are "silly stuff." But that shouldn't mean that Hernandez doesn't think he might have contributed to New York's dramatic come-from-behind victory.

no runs, no hits, no jinx

When Don Larsen of the New York Yankees was on his way to pitching a perfect game against the Brooklyn Dodgers in the 1956 World Series, facing only 27 batters and not permitting a single batter to reach first base, broadcasters who covered the game were very careful to avoid using the terms "no-hitter" or "perfect game" in describing what was happening. They were afraid of jinxing Larsen.

For example, when Larsen came off the mound at the end of the seventh inning, one broadcaster noted that the Yankees had registered "twenty-one straight putouts." Another remarked that "no Dodger has reached first base." But that was as far as they would go.

Today, some players and fans might avoid using the term "no-hitter" when one is in progress, but in broadcasting it's different. "You have to keep people informed today," says Bob Costas, a noted sportscaster. "You have to tell them flat out what's happening."

In 1984, Costas recalls, Vin Scully of NBC-TV covered a game in which Jack Morris of the Detroit Tigers pitched a no-hitter against the Chicago White Sox. "Scully didn't hold back," says Costas. "He told exactly what was going on. He made no effort to avoid the term 'no-hitter.'"

Costas himself covered a near no-hitter in 1982. The pitcher was Charlie Lea of the Montreal Expos, who were playing the Astros in Houston.

"I used the phrase 'no-hitter' at least once every inning," says Costas. "And in the final innings, I did kind of a countdown, saying, 'He's five outs away, he's four outs away, etc.'"

Lea never realized his dream. With two outs in the ninth inning, Terry Puhl of the Astros singled.

Costa scoffs at the idea that he might have jinxed Lea with his openness. He wouldn't think of calling a game any other way. It's "the new reality," he says.

The "new reality" was apparent in 1999 when David Cone of the New York Yankees was in the process of pitching a perfect game against the Montreal Expos. Tim McCarver and Bobby Murcer, broadcasting the game on Fox Television, spoke in clear and direct terms about what was taking place.

According to Richard Sandomir of *The New York Times*, from the bottom of the seventh inning on, McCarver or Murcer said "perfect" nine times and "no-hitter" seven times.

"The curse is officially over," said Sandomir. "Or should be. No announcer should ever fear jinxing a pitcher who is en route to a no-hitter or perfect game by uttering those words before the deed is done."

Swept away

The New York Yankees had just defeated the California Angels in the fourth game of a four-game series, thus completing a series "sweep," as it is called.

As reporters crowded about his locker, Yankee outfielder Claudell Washington held up a good-luck charm that he said had helped the New York team to achieve its sweep. It was a ragged-

looking broom with a long handle. Washington said that a Yankee clubhouse attendant had given the broom to him. "This broom is for four-game sweeps," he said.

Then Washington put the broom aside, poked through his bagful of belongings, and pulled out a whisk broom. "This," he said, holding the small, short-handled broom out in front of him, "is for two-game sweeps."

the fanatic

If there happened to be an All-Star Team of superstitious baseball players, Kevin Rhomberg, an outfielder with the Cleveland Indians, would surely have been a member. Rhomberg believed that it was bad luck if somebody touched him and he didn't touch the person back immediately.

For example, in a game against the Baltimore Orioles, catcher Rick Dempsey accidentally brushed Rhomberg with his glove when he stepped into the batter's box. Rhomberg turned around and touched Dempsey on the arm.

Later in the game, Rhomberg singled. When he was standing on first base, the umpire came over, clapped him on the back and said, "Nice hit." Rhomberg reached out and slapped the umpire on the arm and said, "Thanks."

As Rhomberg took a lead off the base, first baseman Eddie Murray happened to touch him with his glove. Rhomberg darted back to the base, gave Murray a light pat, and then jumped out to take his lead again.

Storm Davis, a pitcher for the Orioles, played on a minor-league team in the Southern League with Rhomberg. Davis played for Charlotte, and Rhomberg for Chattanooga. Davis recalled a game in which Rhomberg was going out to take the field between innings when a Charlotte outfielder on his way to the dugout accidentally bumped against him. Rhomberg chased the man all the way back to the dugout to tag him before he would take his position in the field.

Dave Winfield of the New York Yankees called Rhomberg the most superstitious player in baseball.

But pitcher Charlie Hough of the Texas Rangers had a stronger comment. "That guy's not superstitious," said Hough. "He's nuts!"

psych job

In ice hockey, it's a common practice for players to touch the goalposts and the goaltender's pads with their sticks as pregame warm-ups draw to a close. It's a good-luck gesture. Virtually every player does it.

Craig Ramsey, who had a long career at left wing for the Buffalo Sabres of the National Hockey League, followed that routine—and many others.

Ramsey's rituals began when the Buffalo team was leaving the ice following its warm-up session:

"I'd always go off the ice exactly two minutes before the warm-up ended." Ramsey said. "And just before I'd go, I'd take one shot from the red line and a second shot from the blue line. Rick Seiling [a teammate] was aware of what I always did. So he'd get the puck and pass it to me so I could take those two shots. When it was time to go back out onto the ice, I'd always make it a point to be the next-to-last player to leave the dressing room. Jerry Korab was the player who went out of the dressing room last. He'd let me go ahead of him. When I was back out on the ice and skating around,

I'd make an effort not to cross any of the lines. I always touched the goalie with my stick, too. But I did it in a certain way. I'd tap the ice twice, then tap the goalie twice. Then, when they played the national anthem, I turned sideways, so I kind of faced the other players. Mike Ramsey [another teammate] would tap me with his stick as the anthem played."

Craig, who became Director of Professional Evaluation for the Sabres after he retired as a player, had a reason for his routines. He said:

"You know, I wasn't a great player, a superstar. So what I tried to do was play at the best of my ability as often as possible. I think the superstitions helped. They psyched me up."

the mascot

When John Burkett and Bill Swift each won 20 games for the San Francisco Giants in 1993, it brought back memories of Ron Bryant, another 20-game winner. Bryant posted a 24–12 record in 1973. Bryant, however, is remembered as much for the mascot he carried around with him that season as he is for his pitching skill.

The mascot was a teddy bear. Before he acquired the bear, Bryant was no more than an ordinary pitcher. A lefty from Redlands, California, he had a 5–8 record in 1970 and a 7–10 record in 1971.

In 1972 things began to change. One June afternoon that season, as Bryant was leaving the hotel where the team was staying, he saw a young girl with a teddy bear. Bryant had always been called "Bear" by Mike Murphy, the team's equipment manager. Bryant thought it would be a cute idea to buy the bear and give it to Murphy. He agreed to pay the girl $30 for it.

Bryant took the teddy bear to the ballpark. That afternoon he pitched a neat six-hitter, his best game in weeks. "Maybe it's the bear," he said to himself. "Maybe it brought me good luck."

Bryant began taking the bear everywhere. He sat the bear down next to him on the team bus. He placed it on a stool near his locker stall when he dressed for games. And at home games, the bear was given a seat on the dugout bench.

The bear seemed to work wonders for Bryant. That year he ended up winning 14 games and losing only 7. Bryant was even better in 1973. Whenever he was in a tight spot during a game. Bryant would step off the rubber, then stare over at the bear in the dugout. It was almost as if he gained strength from it. Bryant was the National League's only 20-game winner that season.

Bryant had great expectations for 1974. But before the season opened, he and some teammates were clowning around the swimming pool at the hotel where the team was staying. Bryant fell and injured his hip. Whenever he tried to pitch that year, the hip pained him. He won only 3 games and lost 15. The next year he was pitching in the minor leagues, and the year after that he was out of baseball.

Bryant still cherishes the memories of those two glittering seasons. When asked to explain what happened, he would shake his head and grin. "There were a lot of things involved," he said. "You can't give all the credit to the bear. But the bear sure had something to do with it."

"g" for victory

Pierre Mondou, the popular center of the Montreal Canadiens of the National Hockey League, was known to be one of the most superstitious players on the team. For good luck, Mondou cut the letter "G" on the back edge of all of his hockey sticks. The "G," Mondou said, stood for two words—for "goal" and for "gagner," which is French for "to win."

getting ready

In the locker room before a professional football game, it is usually quiet and tense. Players often use the final moments before going out to the field to indulge in routines that help them to relax.

Guard Tom Nuten of the St. Louis Rams was one of a number of players who followed a formal footwear ceremony when dressing. He always put on his left sock first, then his right sock, then his left shoe, and, last, his right shoe.

Running back Terrell Davis of the Denver Broncos, the Most Valuable Player of Super Bowl XXXII in 1998, had a nametag above his locker like every other player. But Davis insisted that his nametag read "Joe Abdullah."

Drew Pearson, the All-Pro wide receiver for the Dallas Cowboys and a mainstay with the team for more than a decade, spent his time wrapping his shoes in adhesive tape. By the time he was finished, the shoes were completely covered. Not the slightest trace of a brand name or identifying trademark remained.

"I've been offered a lot of money by different shoe companies to show their designs or trademarks," Pearson once said. "But I can't do that. This superstition has been with me for too long a time."

Pearson had another superstitious habit that made him one of the most popular of the Dallas players. Before each game, he'd throw footballs into the stands.

"I'd throw two before each game," he said. "I'd throw them into the end-zone seats to give people there something to look forward to, a souvenir to take with them.

"Coach [Tom] Landry told me not to do it. But I'd sneak a couple in there—and we'd win."

Don Ryczek, a center for the Los Angeles Rams, would begin getting ready for a game by first taking off his shoes and socks and putting on his game shoes (without socks). Then he'd get a cup of coffee and, still in his street clothes, go out to the field. "I'd walk out to the 50-yard line," he once recalled, "turn around, and walk back to the dressing room. Then I'd start getting dressed for the game."

Jim Marshall, a tight end for the Atlanta Falcons, used to tape a penny to each shoe before going out to the field. Claude Humphrey, a defensive end for the team, taped a lucky feather to his helmet.

Place-kicker John Leypoldt of the Buffalo Bills would always spend several minutes polishing his kicking shoe. Tight end Terry Nelson of the Los Angeles Rams taped his fingers before every game, whether they were injured or not.

Doug Betters of the Miami Dolphins always stuck a couple of sticks of gum in his socks as he was getting dressed. "I don't know if that's a superstition," he said, "but I wouldn't take the risk of not doing it."

latin luck

In any discussion of superstitious baseball players, the name of pitcher Mike Cuellar never fails to come up. A pitching star with the Baltimore Orioles from 1969 to 1976, Cuellar's best pitch was a screwball, which is a curveball that breaks the "wrong" way—that is, toward the side from which it was thrown. Those who remember Cuellar agree that he had as many strange habits as strange pitches.

Like many players, Cuellar, who was born in the Dominican Republic, avoided stepping on the foul lines. He also avoided the top step of the dugout. He would always jump over it whenever he left the dugout to go out to the playing field.

On days that he was assigned to pitch, Cuellar refused to sign autographs. And he followed a careful ritual when warming up. Only Jim Frey, a Baltimore coach at the time, was permitted to catch his warmup throws. And teammate Ellie Hendricks had to stand at the plate in a batting stance as Cuellar threw.

During any game in which he pitched, Cuellar would never leave the dugout to warm up for an inning until all his teammates were in their positions on the field.

Cuellar didn't like flying. To ward off bad luck in the air, he always wore blue—a blue shirt, blue jacket, and blue trousers.

Once, when the Orioles were on a road trip, Cuellar unpacked to find that he had failed to take along his baseball cap. He had other caps, but he didn't have the one that he believed brought him good luck.

The Orioles were playing in Milwaukee at the time. A team official called the team's clubhouse in Baltimore and ordered that

Cuellar's cap be put on the next airplane to Milwaukee. After it arrived, the cap was whisked to the ballpark in a taxicab.

In his eight years with the Baltimore team, Cuellar averaged close to twenty wins a season. He won the Cy Young Award one year as the American League's best pitcher. After his career in the major leagues had come to a close, Cuellar, in his mid-forties, continued to pitch in the Dominican Republic. All those years of superstitious practices certainly didn't do him any harm.

tale of the tape

When Reggie Miller was a rookie player with the Indiana Pacers of the National Basketball Association, someone noticed that he had both wrists taped and wore a sweatband over the tape on his left wrist.

If Reggie shot with his left hand, maybe no one would have thought anything about it. But Reggie was normally a right-handed shooter.

How did he explain it?

"The reason I wear tape on my right wrist," he said, "is to help keep my shooting hand straight. I don't want it to flop to the right or left when I shoot.

"I don't wear wristbands on my right arm because they would throw my shot off.

"They're okay on the left wrist. They keep things in balance."

What about the tape on the left wrist? Why wear that?

"I hurt my wrist one time, and I've kept it taped up since," said Reggie. "That's just superstition."

Skipper Superstitions

Most baseball managers are well known for their superstitious practices. Some take the same route to the ballpark every day. Others make it a practice to sit at a certain spot on the bench during the game.

Earl Weaver, who once managed the Baltimore Orioles, practiced several well-known manager superstitions. He always used the same pen to write out the team's lineup card. And he always had the same coach deliver the card to the umpire at home plate before the game.

The Orioles once lost six Sunday games in a row at their home park, Memorial Stadium. To break the jinx, Weaver decided that the team should skip batting practice before the seventh Sunday game. The team won.

"Are you superstitious?" Weaver was often asked. "Naaaah," he'd reply. "That stuff is just fun. It doesn't mean a thing."

His players knew differently. "Fun, my foot," said third basemen Brooks Robinson. "Earl's just as superstitious as any of his players."

looking back

Baseball players of the past were just as superstitious as today's players, perhaps even more so.

The great Babe Ruth, for example, believed that butterflies were bad luck. When he spotted one in the outfield, he'd try to chase it away, a habit that often caused the fans to stare in openmouthed wonder at his strange antics.

Ty Cobb, who played for the Detroit Tigers and is often hailed as the best ballplayer of all time, was very superstitious. Besides observing the usual practices about black cats, rabbits' feet, horseshoes, and the rest, Cobb had several strange habits of his own. When he was on a hitting streak, he always ate the same food and took the same route to the ballpark.

Cobb would not allow his uniform to be cleaned during a hitting streak, no matter how dirty it became. And he once became furious with the team's trainer for moving his shower towel to a different peg from the one on which Cobb had hung it.

Perhaps Cobb's strangest superstition involved the black baseball bat he used in 1907 to hit .350 and win the American League batting crown. He believed the bat carried good luck. Although he never hit with the bat again after 1907, he carried it around with him everywhere. When Cobb was married in August 1908, and he and his bride cut the wedding cake, Cobb did the cutting with his right hand and held the black bat in his left.

paYing the Price

Superstitious routines usually produce shrugs from those who observe them. Nobody cares very much.

But on at least one occasion, a superstitious practice triggered violent brawling. It happened in the minutes before a playoff game between the Montreal Canadiens and Philadelphia Flyers at the Montreal Forum.

The teams had just finished warming up. Almost all the players were off the ice when Montreal forwards Shane Corson and Claude Lemieux each skated into the Philadelphia zone with the idea of shooting a puck into the Flyers' empty net. It was a ritual that Lemieux had observed in four previous games of the series.

Since nearly all the players were off the ice, Lemieux's make-believe goals were hardly noticed.

But the superstitious routine had angered some of the Flyers. As Corson and Lemieux skated toward the Philadelphia net, they were followed by Glenn Resch and Ed Hospodar. As Corson took his shot, Resch slid his stick along the ice toward the puck. Hospodar caught up with Lemieux and started punching him. Lemieux punched back.

Before long, players from both teams were streaming back out onto the ice. The referees, who were still in their dressing rooms, were unaware of what was happening. With no one to hold them back, the players battled for more than ten minutes. There were at least four serious fights besides the original one between Hospodar and Lemieux.

It was a shameful day for ice hockey. An official of the National Hockey League said that the incident "brought dishonor to the league."

The NHL fined the Flyers and Canadiens a total of $24,500 for the brawl. At that price, attempting to shoot a puck into an abandoned net has to rank as one of the most expensive superstitious acts of all time.

Stuffed Superstition

A rabbit's foot is the most popular of all good-luck charms. But Val Skinner, a professional golfer, was not content with a mere foot. Her good-luck charm was a whole rabbit—a whole *stuffed* rabbit, that is.

Skinner received the rabbit as a gift from a friend. When Skinner won the Big Eight golf championship while she was attending Oklahoma State University, she shared the credit with her large-eared pet.

Carrying a stuffed rabbit around a golf course can be awkward. But Skinner solved that problem by having her mother keep the rabbit for her. The fact that the rabbit was at her mom's home in

North Platte, Nebraska, and Skinner was often separated from her furry pet by many hundreds of miles, didn't seem to matter. The rabbit was still able to work its magic.

When Skinner won the MasterCard championship in Westchester County, New York, her third tournament victory as a professional, she again cited the help she had received from the rabbit. "He's gray with brown eyes," she told newspaper and television reporters after her win. "My mom keeps him on the bed back home."

Skinner had a most fitting name for her pet, considering her profession. She called him "One Putt."

golden charms

In the first-ever women's ice hockey competition in the Olympic Games, held in Nagano, Japan, in 1999, the United States captured the gold medal by turning back Canada, 3–1. Good luck played a part in America's stirring victory. Forward Cammi Granato traveled to Japan with her beanbag frog named Floppy. She touched the frog before every game for luck. Goaltender Sarah Tueting always put on her right skate first and wore her brother's old T-shirts.

the hex that failed

After the Denver Broncos had their uniforms redesigned in 1998, they won game after game wearing the new dark-blue jerseys with orange striping. By late January 1999, they had played twenty-one games wearing the new blue shirts, and they had won all of them. They started making preparations to play the Atlanta Falcons in Super Bowl XXXIII.

Then came the announcement that they were to be designated the road team for the Super Bowl, which was to played at Joe Robbie Stadium in Miami. And as the road team, they had to wear their old white jerseys. Many of the players recalled that the team was wearing their white shirts when they suffered their only losses of the season.

Steve Atwater, a defensive back for the Broncos, shrugged off the suggestion that the jersey color had any real meaning. "The uniforms are no big deal," he said.

In the game, the Broncos overcame the Falcons quite easily, 34–19. No one mentioned the jerseys. Steve Atwater was right.

index